Layout by Dinni Astriani: astrianidinni@gmail.com.

Foreword

Why do so many talented individuals fail to reach the heights their skills suggest they could? Matt Anderson has delved deep into this question, and you're about to discover the answers.

Matt articulates the profound impact of desire, guiding readers on how to harness it effectively. He unravels the crucial role that identity plays, adding momentum to our quest for success. The LifePass method, an ingenious mix of reflection and envisioning, seamlessly blends intent with action, powering both the initiation and the often-turbulent journey towards significant achievements.

"Motivation is an Inside Job with Outside Consequences"

By deciphering your power habits through Matt's pointed questions, you'll discover how to blend them into every ambition. Embracing the idea that record breakers consistently maintain records, while others merely guess, you'll learn which metrics matter and how to accurately monitor your progress.

The pivotal "Anchor Moment" solidifies essential attitudes and actions, readying them for action exactly when you need them. And the recounting of Henry's journey? It's a poignant tale that genuinely brought tears to my eyes.

Having written numerous business books and crafted varied multimedia learning materials, I've encountered an abundance of self-help content. Yet, none stirred me to act quite like Matt's insights did.

It's a privilege to write this foreword, presenting Matt's transformative concepts to you. This isn't mere theoretical musings from 'lecture land'. These are tried, tested, and proven strategies grounded in reality.

Each section engages with authentic tales of individuals exemplifying the veracity, potency, and practicality of Matt's teachings. The journey is mapped out – beginning with understanding our starting point, clarifying our destination, and recognising the mental resilience and definitive steps required to realise our desired outcomes.

I'm convinced you'll be as galvanised to act as I was. More than mere action, it's about understanding and executing the right steps at the right moment to achieve what's genuinely right for you.

Dive in! I'm confident you'll be delighted you did. I am.

Peter Thomson

"The UK's Most Prolific Business Development Author"

www.peterthomson.com

Introduction

Because you're reading this, I am going to assume you know you've got a good sales team, and you know they are capable of even more. You genuinely want them to get greater results too. While some of them are doing very well at times, you'd love to see them succeed *consistently* (Chapter 5) and keep growing. Others may have hit a plateau and neither of you are quite sure how to breakthrough it (Chapter 4). Some may have hit a ceiling in their growth and it's an inside job that's required to hit a new growth trajectory (Chapters 1, 3 and 7).

Whatever your noble reasons, take heart in knowing that this is no ordinary content you're holding. The actionable items in each of these chapters can help your advisors get some really significant traction and make some serious mindset shifts to steer your favorite team members into better, sustained improvement.

Essentially, these seven steps are about aligning your identity, dreams, goals, and habits with how you really want to feel and with finding the courage to change. It's easy to understand and inspiring to put into practice.

Recently I was invited to share these seven steps to 1,700 sales professionals in South Korea. As I worked on keeping my head away from nerves and self-doubt, I asked myself: 'Why am I here today? What's important to me to be putting myself through this challenge?' I've always been obsessed with how people can fulfil their potential – isn't that what it's all about?

While if I'm honest, I admit that part of being there was to test myself and see what I was capable of, honestly what drove me most was I wanted people in the audience to act on what I was sharing. I wanted them to experience some of the same joy your advisors can also experience when they start applying the suggestions and processes in this book.

I've written this so you can literally train and coach straight from the exercises in this book. You can share them without having to recreate anything. You can expect your team to have meaningful insights and clear action items to follow through on. It's all taken directly from my 20+ years of consulting with advisors across over a dozen countries. And for those who do the work, they can expect to see some very special outcomes. They are achievers. This is what they do. Let them get on with it!

TABLE OF CONTENTS

THE 7 STEPS
TO 10X YOUR POTENTIAL

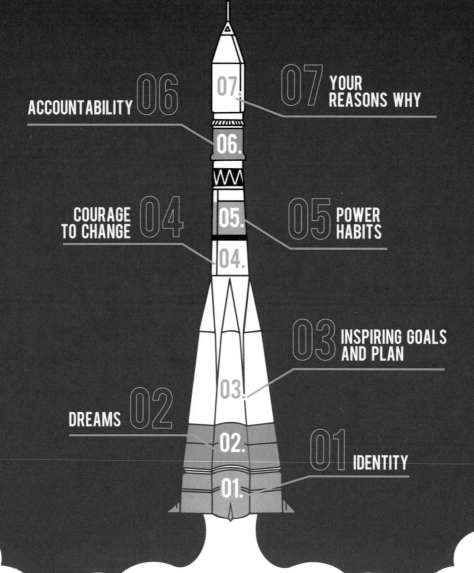

CHAPTER 1

The Rocket Man's Method to Gain the Courage to Perform with Ray Charles

> *"I am God's pencil."*
> *– Mother Teresa*
>
> *"I am a dreamer who never gives up."*
> *– Nelson Mandela*

Shortly after Elton John had released his first album, his manager told him that he was friends with a promoter in the USA who wanted to put a tour together for him to play some club shows. This friend had a good track record and was confident it would be a success.

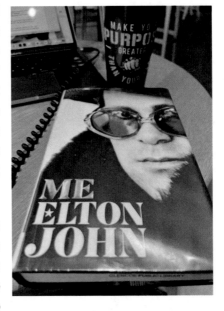

Elton John thought it was a terrible idea. His first album got fantastic reviews, but in his autobiography, *Me*, he adds that it only "crept into the bottom end of the charts." He was convinced it was a bad idea, they would lose the momentum they were getting in the UK, and why go somewhere where no one knew who he was?

Elton lost the argument and a few months later in 1970 at the age of 23, he found himself on the Los Angeles freeway on an old London bus driving him at 40mph from LAX airport to his first venue. While he was touring, the promoter arranged for his first US TV appearance on *The Andy Williams Show*.

He was excited to hear that one of his boyhood idols, Ray Charles, was also going to be on the show. His mind jumped back to being ten at his home in the London suburb of Pinner and singing along in front of the bathroom mirror to one of his records and he looked forward to meeting his hero. The format for the show was for each performer to be interviewed and then perform a song.

But when he arrived at the studio, the producers excitedly told him that they would be performing *together*. They thought it would be a wonderful surprise. But Elton John remembers thinking: *"Ray Charles?* Are you joking? Ray Charles! The Genius? ...some idiot had decided that it was a marvellous idea for him to go on national TV and sing with me, as if a completely unknown English singer-songwriter was kind of a perfect musical counterpart for the man who'd basically single-handedly invented soul music."

But he had no choice. It was his first opportunity to be on US TV. He was in no position to start upsetting American TV executives. He was saved by two things: first, he ignored his emotions, and second, seemingly out of nowhere the thought popped into his head:

I'm a performer.
This is what I do.
Get on with it.

How did it go? "So I got on with it. I don't remember much about the performance itself, but I remember the applause afterwards."

That day Elton John became consciously aware of his identity – of how he saw himself. In his mind, he was a performer. It was unacceptable for him not to be that person and do what that type of person does. That day it gave him the necessary courage and over his lifetime, it has served him majestically for over 50 years!

Why is this such a big deal for the business growth of each advisor on your team? Their identity – how each of them sees themselves – dictates *all the results they get.*

Do they want to grow personally or professionally and get up to bigger and better things in life?

If they want better results in any area of their life, **their identity – how they see themselves- must align because, as my business mentor Peter Thomson says:**

> **"People will never consistently DO who they aren't."**

Let me prove it to you.

a) **This is an exercise to run with your team.** Ask them:

> "Which areas of your life generally go well: Health, certain key relationships, love, your vocation, financial, and/or spiritual area?
>
> Unless you've just experienced a majorly challenging life event (I still remember when my wife and I had twins in our 40's), there are usually at least 2-3 areas - whether it's how you run your business, maintain certain relationships, or perhaps take care of your health."

Share an example: "Let's say you expect to have very good relationships with your top clients (or children). If for some reason, there's a disagreement about something with one of them, quite soon you will do everything you can to make sure that relationship is going well again because it's unacceptable for you. Even if you do it all unwittingly, you make these changes for the better. It works like a thermostat. You readjust based on the 'temperature' of that area. You consistently do the 'right' things in this life area to make sure you usually get good results."

Starting with their life areas, have them write this out:

I AM...

1. **e.g.** a good (vocation)
2. **e.g.** a good parent/son/daughter/sister/brother/friend etc.
3. **(leave blank)**
4. Good with my (health/financial/spiritual)
5. (character trait) Friendly, kind, good listener, intelligent, achiever, heart-led etc.

This is really important to engrain with them. These good outcome areas are a part of almost everyone's identity. We EXPECT good outcomes, and we make sure they go well *most of the time.*

It is unacceptable for us not to get good results in that area.

Now I want you to understand The Dilts' Pyramid because it outlines how results happen in your life and for your advisors.

From top to bottom:

1.   **Identity - I am...**
2.   **Beliefs - I believe...**
3.   **Skills - I can...**
4.   **Actions - I do...**
5.   **Results - I have...**

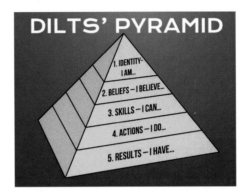

All your outcomes (5) come from what you do (4) and the skills you have to do the actions (3), but they only happen *consistently* when you believe (2) that they are part of who you are as a person (1). In other words, your results *begin with your identity and how you see yourself.*

If you want the advisors on your team to be top producers, the FIRST thing for them to clarify and focus on – as with Elton John – is to say:

1.   I am a top performer.
2.   I believe I have earned it to be a top performer (or: that this is who I was born to be)
3.   I am capable of doing what top performers do.
4.   I do the things consistently that top performers do, so
5.   I have the results that top performers get.

Now are you clear that *how your advisors see themselves* matters is crucial?

Once your advisors have identified the strong areas of their identity, you want them to think about an area of their life where they're not happy with the outcomes – hopefully their business! They have an identity for this area too but it's not as empowering as they need it to be. It may all be subconscious, but that identity is something more along the lines of:

- I am not a top performer
- I am not very good at saving money
- I am not in good shape
- I am in a mediocre relationship that brings little joy

b) Ask them: "Which areas of your life do you want to change for the better?"

Start to think about the type of person you want to be (that you aren't yet)

- Brave
- Free
- Generous
- Grateful
- Confident
- Consistent
- A leader
- Versatile
- Advocate
- Conduit for money or love
- Focused
- Organised
- Accomplished

Tell them to create an inspiring list. Ideally *blend it in* with who they already are that already does a good job. It makes it easier for their brains to buy in.

c) You can encourage them to add to their identity list. "Think about character traits that describe you by adding some: Friendly, kind, good listener, intelligent, achiever, heart-led etc."

"You might also add personal descriptors:

Good cook, (your team) fan, movie lover, musician, loves to learn, nationality or city native etc."

How else do they instil this new identity so that they bolster their belief, refine their skills, do what they need to do and get the results they want? Read on – all 7 steps can help and, if they want great new breakthrough results, developing a new empowered identity is crucial.

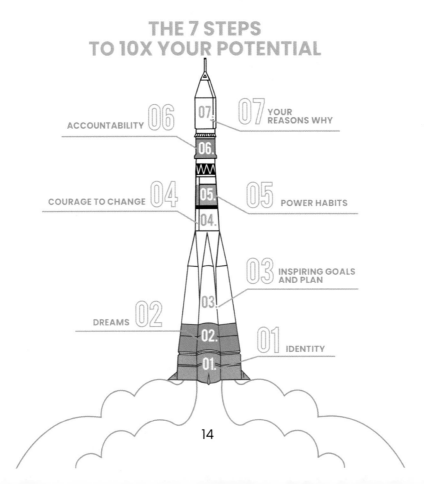

THE 7 STEPS
TO 10X YOUR POTENTIAL

ACCOUNTABILITY 06

07 YOUR REASONS WHY

COURAGE TO CHANGE 04

05 POWER HABITS

03 INSPIRING GOALS AND PLAN

DREAMS 02

01 IDENTITY

CHAPTER 2

The Little-Known Advice From a 13ᵗʰ Century Persian Poet

> *"Dreams are the seeds of change. Nothing ever grows without a seed, and nothing ever changes without a dream."*
> - Debby Boone
>
> *"Dreams are not what you see in your sleep; dreams are things which do not let you sleep."*
> – A.P.J. Abdul Kalam

Two years ago, I met Dawn, a private banker at a large Canadian bank who lives in Chicago. I can honestly say that she is the most enthusiastic banker I have ever met. When I commented: "you really seem to enjoy your work," she told me her story: "I used to be a hairdresser and, while there's nothing wrong with that and I enjoyed working with people, I felt like I wanted a bigger challenge. So, I applied to  work at a bank as a relationship manager. I knew I had the people skills; I just didn't know about finance. That was 20 years ago, and I still love what I do."

I was curious where else she might want to go in life, so I asked her what her goals were over the next 1-5 years. She said: **"I feel like I'm living my dream."** This really took me aback because, well – how often do you hear someone say this and they're not actually trying to be funny?! When I asked her what her key was to her professional accomplishments, she said: "I don't believe in customer satisfaction...

I am someone who believes in customer delight."

The first place your advisors need to support their identity is to connect it with their dreams.
Dreaming is not just for children.

I think it's sad that there's some stigma to the concept. It's foolish too: Think of leaders such as Dr Martin Luther King, Jr who literally proclaimed: "I have a dream!"

Many change agents in countries throughout our world and our history had dreams of freedom and equality. They did not give up on their dreams once they turned 18. They knew what was right in their hearts for their people and for humankind. Nelson Mandela spent 27 years in prison and was 72 years old before he could act on his dream! Most of us have abandoned our new year's resolutions by the third week of January!!

Do you see dreamless 9-5ers wishing everyone a happy 'hump day' on Wednesdays who are hanging on the walls of any art gallery, performing opera, or playing their hearts out at concert houses or band venues? Performers and artists have pursued dreams since the beginning of time. How does your favourite song make you feel? Writers didn't settle for their day job. They dreamed their work could make a difference to somebody.

Many accomplished entrepreneurs have wanted to make the world a better place by solving a problem they had. They turned it into a business that solved that problem or shared that passion with others. ***Why can't your advisors have the same sense of purpose? No human soul on this planet is any better than them. Don't let them *choose* that as their excuse.***

If you have advisors who are plateauing, stuck or who feel alone or fighting against biased forces, when was the last time they dreamed? The mistake too many people make is not to take their dreams seriously. That only leads one way! In his wonderful book, *The Dream Manager*, Matthew Kelly reminds us:

We all need dreams to chase if we are to avoid empty, flat lives.

Oprah Winfrey believes we should all take the time to dream. She describes it beautifully as a *process* of continually seeking to be better, challenging yourself to pursue excellence on every level. And when you do this, you get one step closer to your dreams.

It may not include wealth or fame but has "everything to do with creating a life filled with
Joy
No regrets and
A clear conscience."

I love her perspective because she has met so many highly accomplished people. They don't all become billionaires or famous, but a lifetime of joy sounds extremely good to me.

Two ways Oprah describes her identity are "I am: A woman in progress" (at age 69) and "I live inside God's dream for me."

Regardless of your spiritual beliefs, isn't that inspiring? How could you not want to make the most of your time on earth?

How do your advisors identify their dreams?
13th century Persian poet Rumi says it best:

Last night
I begged the Wise One to tell me
the secret of the world.
Gently, gently, he whispered,
"Be quiet,
the secret cannot be spoken,
It is wrapped in silence."

In other words: Relax. Breathe. Be silent. Listen to the still, small voice.

Encourage them to *ease* back into dreaming if they haven't done it in a while but don't skip this step because it feels like a luxury activity. In fact, you might well want them to dream MORE OFTEN because their dreaming muscles are so weak and flabby. Urge them to find at least twenty silent minutes on their own (put headphones on if they have to) and answer this:

If a genie showed up and waved a magic wand to create your ideal life, here's what would happen today and beyond...

They must *feel* it: Suggest they start with a stream of consciousness writing with no judgement from their egos. Let them form an ever-clearer picture of what they really want. Have them catch any thinking when their brains start to wonder (worry?) how they're going to make it happen. It's totally normal for their brain to go there, but it's too soon. Feeling good matters. It instils them with hope and optimism.

Point out that they haven't written down anything that isn't possible, have they? No one writes: 'grow another six inches,' 'win an Olympic gold in gymnastics,' or 'become a European monarch'.

I am not going to be cruelly optimistic in this book and you won't want to fall into that trap either. They will not easily achieve every dream with a hack or three simple steps. The value to dreaming is to give them a vision, to fuel them with more mental and physical energy to keep trying new ways and keep scaling new mountains so they spend their life seeing what they are really made of. Of not succumbing to a life of quiet desperation.

I'm guessing they want to make a lot more money. You and I do too, because we – probably like them - have a family to love on and many people we want to contribute to. But we must remind ourselves as we dream that while money can solve some problems and afford some more opportunities, it does not bring happiness. As Oprah advises based on the *many* people she has interviewed in her lifetime, **go for joy.**

My all-time favourite question is:
What would you do if you knew you couldn't fail?

I don't know if you can have your advisors ask themselves this too often. Also consider posing this question from *The Dream Manager*:

"Isn't one of the primary responsibilities of all relationships to help each other fulfil our dreams?"

This begs the question: are they clear not only about their dreams but the dreams of their loved ones? Their partner and children? *What about their top clients?* I suspect many of us fall at the first hurdle here (ourselves!).

Start by dreaming. It's not just for children and the ultra-high net worth. You deserve to do this too; it will support your new identity, your advisors' new identities AND it will take you all further on your rising stardom journey.

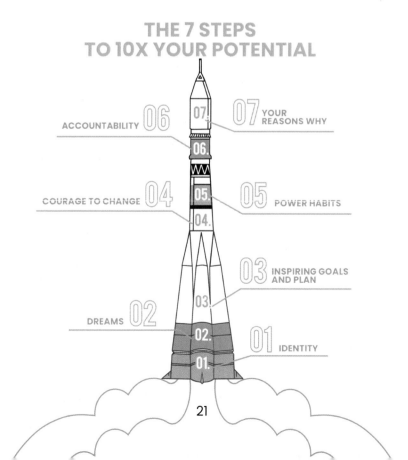

THE 7 STEPS
TO 10X YOUR POTENTIAL

ACCOUNTABILITY 06

07 YOUR REASONS WHY

COURAGE TO CHANGE 04

05 POWER HABITS

03 INSPIRING GOALS AND PLAN

DREAMS 02

01 IDENTITY

CHAPTER 3

The $1bn App Founder's Way to Success

> *"The best and most beautiful things in the world cannot be seen or even touched. They must be felt with the heart."*
> *-Helen Keller*
>
> *"Feeling and longing are the motive forces behind all human endeavour and human creations."*
> *- Albert Einstein*

Payal Kadakia's parents ran away from India in the 1970's to get married. She grew up as the only, brown-skinned girl in her community in New Jersey. She was often teased, told she was "not one of us" by her classmates, and throughout her school years lived a "life divided" between the U.S. and Indian sides of her life.

"There were days when I told my mom I didn't want to go back to school. I felt like I didn't fit in," she says.

Luckily when she was young, she did get to taste something magical and that was dance. "When I danced and felt that feeling, I felt like the most authentic version of me." And she wasn't referring to the physical feeling. It was how it connected her to and inspired others. In her autobiography *Lifepass*, she writes: "I could use dance…as a vehicle to move other people." She loved watching the latest Bollywood videos on VHS with "the emotive women and their intricate dance steps."

"Nothing else in my life could compare to it and once I uncovered that, I always wanted to feel that in anything I did," she says. That feeling was her "anchor." After getting her degree at MIT, she chose the safe option of business consulting in New York because "that would make my parents proud" and lived happily earning $150,000.

The turning point came when her friend, Parul, invited her to her birthday party in San Francisco in 2010. "On a WHIM (author's emphasis), I decided to go, and the trip became a life-altering lesson in how getting a change of pace and gaining some distance can sometimes be exactly what we need to gain perspective."

While chatting with the guests, she found herself surrounded by a completely different group of people unlike her business friends in New York. They were "developing apps, starting companies or embarking on some type of entrepreneurial journey."

On the flight back her mind raced with inspiration. She said to herself: "I'm going to take two weeks to see if I can think of an idea. If I can think of an idea I really care about, maybe this is worth it."

Two days later she was looking for a ballet class online and failing miserably – with 30 open tabs on her computer. It led to her realizing that she had her own need to fill which was to create an app that helped people find and book health-related classes. Through various challenging iterations, it became ClassPass which just nine years later was valued at

$1 billion. She became the first woman of colour business founder to achieve this.

Kadakia definitely had a clear sense of purpose. In her words, "I was following my calling and marching to work fuelled with the passion to make a difference in the world."

However, after three years as an entrepreneur she definitely didn't have a life that she enjoyed: "I started to recognize that maybe I had gone too far." She had been on holiday to Hawaii and, on the flight back, sadly admitted to herself that work had taken over her life. "Classpass...was something I poured all my time and energy into." Life felt "unpredictable", "unhealthy" and she felt "incredibly alone."

Right there on the plane **she developed a new way to set inspiring goals based on how she wanted to *feel*.** This is brilliant because much of what we strive to achieve is unwittingly centred on how that makes us feel - yet we rarely make that connection. We all want to feel successful, but we seldom define what that means to us. If we take the time to listen to the still, small voice inside, we learn that it's not all about the money.

Kadakia asked herself where she wanted to be in a year's time and how she wanted to feel. Then she distilled this down to what she calls five dream words. From these words, she set her priority life areas and created some measurable, 12-week goals to target. In her book she calls this her Lifepass Method.

The inspiring part is that when you look at your (yes, very practical looking) goals this way, you see the direct path to how you want to feel about different areas of your life. If you're someone who wants to follow your heart in life, this process will have far more impact than ideas purely from your logical, rational (often a lot less inspired) brain.

Inspiring goals are crucial to bring your advisors' new identities into reality.

They will fuel them on the often long and challenging journey of the high achievement you want. **Their brains require proof that they are doing the work to become the type of person they want to be.** This takes a lot of repetition and is another reason New Year's Resolutions rarely stand a chance.

One big mistake too many aspiring rising stars make is they don't tune into their hearts when they set goals and instead settle for emotionally flat targets that tick a box rather than stir the soul.

I am not being fanciful with this observation: They are going to feed their families a lot better when they are fuelled with inspiration rather than 'required targets' and at risk of living in a survival (lower) state of mind versus an executive (inspired) one (see Chapter 4).

Here's a quick reminder for your advisors of the five reasons goals matter so much:

a) Best benefit: **they know where they're going.** When they do, they get there more quickly. Goals can provide the steps.
b) They help with FOCUS: Their brain can only handle seven bits of information at once.
c) Goals help them realise their ambitions.
d) Goal-orientated people put more effort into accomplishing their goals.
e) Goals make decisions easier and help them avoid whims and moods.

Set Inspiring Goals Based on Your Feelings Using the Lifepass Method

Talk your advisors through these TWO BIG steps:

STEP ONE: SET THE GOALS

a) Reflect on the past 12 months.

Write down words that describe the past year in terms of the feelings, themes, thoughts, high and low points that come to mind. Let your mind ponder what happened with your key relationships, health, vocation, finances, love, and spiritual life. After this, pick the five strongest words that summarise your past year.

e.g., Purposeful, inconsistent, frustrated, caring, blocked (= a mix of the good things and the difficulties)

b) Think ahead 12 months: What do you hope will have happened?

First list out those outcomes and then identify the *feeling* behind them.

How will you feel if you can increase revenues by x% or get back in good shape again?

Select the top five from this list of feelings.

Pick the most inspiring word you can use to anchor to your goal.

e.g., Confident, focused, leader, enthusiastic, impactful, brave, following my heart.

c) Prioritise the top 5 areas you want to focus on in the next 12 weeks.

This is a smart idea. You can't work on everything at once. This helps you prioritise your time, money, and energy. And not spread you too thin. List all the different areas of your life. You can add areas that don't exist but that involve important things you want to start. Often excluded areas are passions, hobbies, friends, and self-care.

You can also add more than one role in an area if it really needs the attention, e.g., two roles at work, two areas of health, family, or finances. Then score them all **on a scale of 1-10 "in terms of whether or not that specific part of your life is currently moving you in the direction of your dream words."**

d) What could you DO in the next 12 weeks to start feeling that way?

While your dream words are the focus and targets for the 12 months, the focus areas and goals might change each quarter. Brainstorm some ideas.

e.g., Launch a new marketing campaign, swim more, start meditating, call your family more, promote product A again etc.

e) Make the goals measurable.

i. Pick no more than **three 12-week goals** per area. **Make them SMART Goals:** Specific, Measurable, Achievable, Realistic, Time-Bound

I earn $x by Dec 31, 20xx

I weigh x lbs./kg by June 30, 20xx

I enjoy x date nights with my partner/children per month

ii. **10X your goals and write these out daily.**

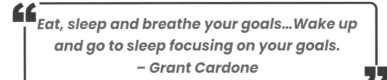

Eat, sleep and breathe your goals...Wake up and go to sleep focusing on your goals.
– Grant Cardone

Entrepreneur Grant Cardone is a huge advocate for setting goals that are out of reach for today and 10x-ing your goals to get you excited and taking massive action (versus average). Write these in the present tense. Avoid focusing right away on the 'how' part but on the excitement. If you want your advisors to achieve the outstanding, they must be doing the opposite of average.

> *To live great, you have to think big.*
> *– Gary Keller*

You don't know what you are capable of unless you set an inspiring and ambitious feeling: Big is not bad. It may cause some fear and worthiness questions but answer this: **"Do you know what your limits are?"** No, you don't.

STEP TWO: C.I.A. Plan – CREATE INSPIRED ACTIONS Plan

Once you have your goals, you need a plan that involves ideally as close to 10X actions as you can manage (without sacrificing your health or family relationships)! To be fair, how else can you legally 10X your potential without really doing what others are unwilling to do?

The best way to do this is by using a process developed by my mentor, the UK's best-known business and personal growth strategist, Peter Thomson and his Yesterday's Road Method.

a) Picturing one of your 10X goals with a timeline, put yourself at that end date NOT having achieved the goal. Really, truly, FEEL the PAIN of this FAILURE.

b) Then take a pen and paper and write as much as you can in response to: **"IF ONLY I'd…"**

You have to take ownership for your failure and think about ALL the things you should/could have done.

c) Then picture the future differently. You DID achieve the goal. Let that joy sink in. Then take a pen and paper and write as much as you can to explain that you DID achieve the goal: **"Because I..."** and add NEW ideas.

d) **Prioritise all the ideas from your TWO lists.**
   The key here is NOT TO EDIT your lists of actions and start removing suggestions. You want to keep all the inspired ones even if the light of day makes them look too intimidating.

Lastly, tread carefully about who you tell

There are two opposite camps on this one – you decide!

a) Keep them to yourself because telling others can give you the feeling it's already been achieved. It might dilute your efforts or open you up to naysayers who fill you with self-doubt and prompt you to talk yourself out of it.

b) Tell the whole world and you'll be too embarrassed not to achieve it – you've stuck your neck out and committed yourself. I've seen this work on social media with a former client who wanted to lose a lot of weight.

I hope you can make this a fun exercise for your advisors and don't forget they can always modify their goals. Every 12 weeks, they can revisit which areas they need to focus on and which goals they set understanding that the end goal is to feel a certain way at the end of the 12 months.

The journey will always be a curve that goes up and down. I love these steps and they can also start to reinforce their new identities, set them up for success on their terms, give them the focus they need, and the inspiration to make their next 12 months their best yet!

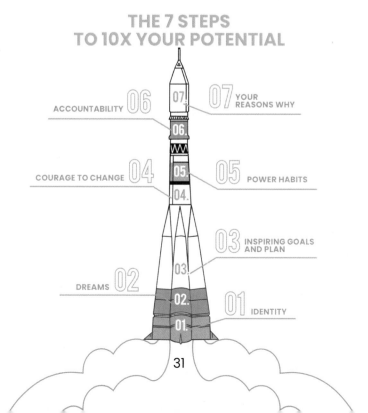

THE 7 STEPS
TO 10X YOUR POTENTIAL

ACCOUNTABILITY 06   07   07 YOUR REASONS WHY

06.

05.

COURAGE TO CHANGE 04   05 POWER HABITS

04.

03 INSPIRING GOALS AND PLAN

03.

DREAMS 02

02.   01 IDENTITY

01.

CHAPTER 4

The Process from Amputation to Purposeful Leadership

> "No matter what has occurred in your life up to this point, it should have no bearing at all on how you live from now on."
> – Alfred Adler
>
> "Don't wait for someone else to come and speak for you. It's you who can change the world."
> - Malala Yousafzai

Ana Daniela Morosanu (Dani) grew up in communist Romania taking the Pioneer Oath and wearing the uniform of the 'father of the fatherland' - Nicolae Ceausescu's Pioneers. On her first day of school when she was seven years old, she was in a car accident that resulted in a third of her lower right leg being amputated. "My life with an amputation was so challenging that I just desired a simple life."

However, partly because of the high expenses associated with her prosthetic needs, she decided to go into sales at the age of 25. Over the next fifteen years she did well as a manager and won several awards, but it felt soulless. "I was trying to please my bosses and I was helping them achieve their dreams, but not my own. I wanted my work to serve a greater purpose, but my bosses were only interested in me hitting my numbers." Essentially, she was living someone else's life.

In 2017 at the age of 40, she hit a wall when her lifetime of repressed anger from all that had happened to her welled up so much that it expressed itself physically as an infection that spread up her entire leg. It was as if her body couldn't take it anymore and was screaming: "Help! Come up with a better solution to bottling up your anger and your dreams!"

She couldn't wear her prosthesis and was bedridden for four months. For the first two weeks her body trembled - not in fear but in anger.

She had to pay attention now. "I felt a fire within me. I needed to align my inner self with the external world. I remember that day when, after crying for an hour, I finally gave in to my own stubbornness and **started listening to my heart.** I said, 'Alright, God! I wholeheartedly accept what is destined for me! I won't resist anymore!' And since then, amazing things have been happening."

This experience began the uncomfortable process for Dani to find the courage to change.

Making these changes is a winnable long-term game for your advisors when you know how they can address their own obstacles.

Helping Your Advisors Find the Courage to Change. Talk them through these steps:

1. **ACCEPT what life is trying to teach you and accept yourself.**

   It's not easy to accept something you don't like or don't want but this was the first realisation Dani had during the four months she was bedridden with her leg infection.

   We create a lot of noise and distraction to hide from our pain. David Goggins learned this from his life and made this point in *Can't Hurt Me*:

   ### *"Denial is the ultimate comfort zone."*

   Dani had to stop denying what she could not change and what wasn't working. You do too. This frees you up to focus on what you can change.

2. *Accept* **the pain then filter it out:**

   Dani had to let go of her anger because it had literally made her sick.

   TALK it out

   WALK it out

   WRITE it out

   BREATHE it out

   Whatever works best for you. Just be conscious that the pain is exiting – that there is a surrender process.

Be *much* kinder to yourself – as *consistently* as you can. Achiever types are especially prone to being overly hard on themselves and it is seldom helpful. When you talk to yourself the way you would a close friend, when you practice self-care and self-love, this all adds up. It sends the brain more empowering messages that you are precious cargo.

3. **Decide: It's Not What You Are Born with But What You Make of Your Equipment** (Alfred Adler paraphrase)

What happened to you in the past does influence you, but it does not have to determine your future otherwise every single person on the planet who has a similar challenge from their past (e.g., grew up with a highly critical parent) would grow up to have the exact same outcomes. **But they don't, do they?** Those labelled as 'resilient' go on to do astonishing things.

Arnold Schwarzenegger grew up with a very critical father. In his autobiography *Total Recall* he writes: *"I never felt that I was good enough, strong enough, smart enough. A lot of sons would have been crippled by his demands, but instead the discipline rubbed off on me. I turned it into drive...*

"Every time he (my father) hit me, every time he said my weight training was garbage, it put fuel on the fire in my belly."

It's interesting that Schwarzenegger says he probably would never have left Austria if his father had been kind, gentle and loving, and he would likely never have had the drive to achieve what he did without his dad's criticism.

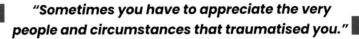

"Sometimes you have to appreciate the very people and circumstances that traumatised you."

He deserves our applause. How many people think like this and empower themselves after an abusive or challenging past?

In other words, decide that you can change too: **You have the ability! Now you need to find the courage...**

4. **Choose Positive Meanings for the Areas of Your Life That Get Disappointing Results.**

Think about one of those areas: When you bring up bad memories about it or tell yourself the same story over and over, you are assuring that this area will usually go badly. Unwittingly, you have a GOAL to do badly in that area. Because you 'choose' to bring up a bad memory, story or thought, you are chained and controlled by the past. Isn't that scary?

In the brilliant Japanese bestseller, *The Courage to Be Disliked*, authors Ichiro Kishimi and Fumitake Koga explain that when you use past misfortune as a reason or excuse, you will always need it again – that if you focus on past causes, *you will take NO steps forward*. The meaning you give something will always determine your outcomes.

If you want to regain control of any area of your life, you must choose *not* to bring up disempowering thoughts (see these stories/beliefs/reasons/excuses as terminal cancer cells) and instead choose to attach a wildly powerful, positive meaning to this area from now on.

Decide to use your past for whatever suits *your* purposes rather than live on an unhelpful autopilot!

For example, Dani was struggling professionally to find purpose to her work and her repeat-cycle thinking was: **"I find it hard to** feel anything other than alone - no one else wants what I want. If my team does not share the same goal and vision as me, it is hard to achieve a big dream" – so she continued to feel soulless.

After her leg infection, she chose a positive, different meaning:

"I am a role model for those who feel alone and without a team to support their vision.

My purpose/destiny in life is to find the right team with the right values to protect 100,000 families with 100 advisors." This is how she found purposeful leadership.

Now come up with your own examples: If you're struggling professionally and/or have felt on a plateau for some time, your repeat-cycle thinking is: **"I find it hard to** get past the roadblocks I keep hitting."

Choose a positive, different meaning and feel free to use this format for your new thinking:

"I am a role model for those who are stuck in business; I've been there.

My purpose/destiny in life is to scale my business increasingly on an upward trajectory because I am a caring, intelligent person of integrity who is hard-wired for purpose-centric work and consistent growth – and I can mentor others to do the same."

(This is who I am. Get on with it – remember that?!)

If you've almost always struggled with being fit and healthy, your repeat cycle thinking is: **"I find it hard to** be in shape."

Choose a positive, different meaning to this life area:

"I am a role model for those who are out of shape; I've been there for far too long.

My purpose/destiny in life is to be fit and healthy and to feel strong and energised – and help others do the same."

This step is the most important of all in pushing you to find the courage to change.

Face your fear and rewrite your future now.

Your past does not have to determine your future if YOU *commit* **not to let it!!!**

If you need one more reason to create new inspired meaning from past misfortune, I'm not sure it can be put any better than this:

In Italy, for 30 years under the Borgias, they had warfare, terror, murder, and bloodshed, but they produced Michelangelo, Leonardo da Vinci, and the Renaissance.

In Switzerland, they had brotherly love, they had 500 years of democracy and peace – and what did that produce? The cuckoo clock. Orson Welles as Harry Lime in The Third Man (1949)

- **In other words, your hardship can teach you something and lead to making your life your own work of art.**

5. **Learn to Shut the Duck Up! Catch your fear-based inner critic duck quacking away in your head. All Day!**

You can't stop your human brain from having doubts, opinions, and fears. It's the first thing that will happen *after* you write down your new meanings. **The highest achievers learn how to filter out these unhelpful thoughts and memories better than everyone else.**

In his book, *Solve for Happy,* former Chief Business Officer at Google (X) Mo Gawdat recommends finding ways to "Shut the Duck Up" in your head by observing all the tiny details around you or pay close attention to your body or breathing – "something *other than thought*...(to) reduce (your brain's) ability to engage in useless thoughts." It can feel uncomfortable, but "you are not the voice in your head...(you) don't have to listen to that duck anymore."

6. **Pick Which of the Two Brain States You Want to Live In: Survival or Executive State.**

I heard this recently from Dr Eugene Choi when I was attending one of branding expert Mike Kim's in-person mastermind group meetings.

Survival State

The average person spends 70% of their time in survival state which includes fight, flight and freeze states. Before you think that doesn't cover much for you:

Fighting for survival has obvious tendencies such as arguing, being angry and road rage but also includes hustling, trying to prove yourself, people pleasing, needing to be right, the need for control (OCD anyone?), people pleasing, judging and perfectionism.

Fleeing for survival has the obvious traits such as quitting and literally escaping a problem but also **includes numbing (escaping) behaviours**. You tend to do these unwittingly and they include over-eating, drinking, drugs, sex, television/video games, and gambling.

When I think about my own addictive tendencies, it can include other activities that don't get talked about much such as over-exercising and my biggest numbing behaviour is also one of my greatest strengths – learning. When I am frustrated at my lack of results, I am often afraid it's my ignorance about a topic and I think, "Oh I must find the answers in a book I haven't read yet or need to re-read because I missed the 'key' point."

One of the mistakes I used to make was to think that most (not all) of my addictive numbing tendencies were socially acceptable – like working too hard and too much (I pretended not to acknowledge that the symptoms of workaholism are the same as alcoholism!). That cultural influence and my inability to tune into how I was really feeling led to years of living in denial about my frustrations and areas of my life where I wasn't seeing the results I wanted.

Freeze behaviours include procrastination and all forms of inaction.

Executive state… is where you want to be!!!

This includes activities of creativity, intuition, inspiration, empathy, and problem solving. You are in a state of flow such that you are not focused on yourself but on serving the world by doing something a little challenging that you love to do and are good at.

What to Do:

You don't need to keep fighting and avoiding your frustrations.

First, **just accept them** and avoid going into survival activities because one thing is certain: **they will never go away if you do that.**

Second, you will also want to increase your tolerance for the pain first (otherwise you will just numb it again).

Trust that by leaning into the discomfort, you will come out the other side and the discomfort will subside.

Third, start asking yourself on the inside: **"What would feel like a more executive activity?"**

Fourth, you might need to have some fun first, or you might need to slow down and make more time to relax instead of always hustling. Mark Black reminds us that: *"Sometimes the most productive thing you can do is relax."* Our culture seems to have forgotten this as a human need.

Fifth, you need the right environment to flourish. You want people around you cheering you and steering you on to accomplish that. It's an increasingly lonely world out there for too many people that now even governments (in Japan and the UK) are recognising this as a social epidemic by creating Departments of Loneliness.

In May 2023 the US Surgeon General announced that loneliness was more perilous to your health than smoking 15 cigarettes a day or air pollution. It's time to build yourself a stronger community. That's why I created one; we do better when supported by like-minded people. If this resonates at all, ask me about the private company page option at my app community: https://community.bearisingstar.com

Changing your behaviours is not as easy as being aware of them (unfortunately) because by the time you are in your mid-thirties, 95% of what you do is done on autopilot. I wrote about this in my last book, *The 5 Habits to Mine Your Gold*. Having spent a lifetime falling into these ruts myself, I know these roads. One way I help my clients is to establish new habits and beliefs to move away from these traps.

This is how you start to let your frustrations know that they are being heard and you can dilute them down versus fighting them. Rather like the over-quoted line from Einstein – you won't be solving any of your problems at the same level you created them. It's time to leave that state!

Ana Daniela Morosanu
Metropolitan Life Romania
Romania

7. **Align**

The purpose of the 7 Steps to Rising Stardom is to align each step for you so that there is a congruence to everything you do. It starts with your identity, then your dreams, and having goals that inspire you based on how you most want to feel.

When You Listen to and Are Led by Your Heart, You Can Find More Courage to Change

This was a key lesson for Dani: "Now I let my HEART speak and my BRAIN assist it." It was only when she tuned into what her heart really wanted that she realised that she had suppressed a lot of anger by trying too hard to please her bosses instead of doing what was most important to her. Only then did she truly get into action.

It's a balance: it's great to love on the people who matter most to you, and much of your happiness will come from contributing to your 'community' and focusing on the concerns of others – but you also need to take care of yourself so you can be there for others!

8. **Connect With Your Higher Power**

Just as Dani surrendered to God to stop resisting what she couldn't change and accept her destiny by listening to her heart, if it helps you to be your best self:

There is nothing more powerful than having the audacious belief that the Universe has got your back.

When you can face your biggest challenges and feel a wave of support inside you – *that you are not alone at all* - it's a very powerful feeling. It can also provide you with a much-needed boost of **patience** and **courage** before the results appear and, sometimes, we need all the help we can get.

Can you believe that there is a power who wants you to fulfil your destiny? It's not easy to go this deep but as Fiona Harrold says: *"Here's the secret to the quest for deep and lasting self-belief. You can choose to believe anything you want."*

Your Role Models Can Deliver Courage Too

Recently when I had a big speech to make in Seoul to 1700 financial service professionals and was seeking more courage, I pulled out my computer to look up the exact words Stephen Covey had used when responding to a question I had asked him about Victor Frankl at a live event in Seattle once. He had said: **"You can choose your beliefs. You can do anything you set your mind to."**

What would your role model/s say to empower you?

Lastly, when you listen closely enough, there is a voice there telling you that you have the ability, and it is okay for you to shine.

9. **Get into Action and Stay in Action**

   You need to PROVE to your brain that you are becoming the type of person you want to be and that you are overcoming your old limiting meanings and memories by taking action towards your dreams and goals.

   If you lean into the belief that you are making a positive contribution to your world, it raises your worthiness and can give you the courage to change and keep taking further steps.

10. **Gradually Increase Your Trajectory Out of Your Comfort Zone 4% At a Time**

    You also know you can't keep doing the same thing over and over and expect new results. As you take more action and set more 12-week goals to prove to your brain that you are living into your new meaning, you will likely need to gradually increase the difficulty or scale of what you're doing.

    4% is an arbitrary number suggested by peak performance expert Steven Kotler. You don't want to throw yourself into a panic zone, but you do want to get out of the prison of your comfort zone and build your courage muscle. This could be targeting slightly bigger prospects, doing small public speaking gigs, and/or taking on greater physical challenges. **It's the cumulative nature of what you do that matters:**

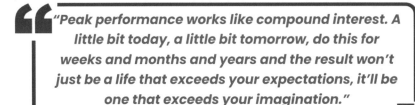

> *"Peak performance works like compound interest. A little bit today, a little bit tomorrow, do this for weeks and months and years and the result won't just be a life that exceeds your expectations, it'll be one that exceeds your imagination."*
> – Steven Kotler, The Art of Impossible

This also builds flow state. Flow requires some degree of challenge to engage you positively and the more flow activities you can stack, the more productive you become.

11. Continue to Shut the Duck Up!!!

There is never a point in life when your ego stops trying to scare you, so this point has to be revisited more than you'd like.

Pick the meaning and beliefs you want. It won't be easy but persist and know it to be true. And be part of a bigger community that is doing this now! My new app community is here to provide a bigger support team to where you want to go and has the option for private company pages:

🔍 | https://community.bearisingstar.com

12. See Yourself as Advantaged: Choose to Believe that Your Whole Life Has Been Happening FOR You Not TO You.

We all have our demons, and we all have beliefs that limit us. What Dani did so remarkably was to decide to look at her past pain, change the meaning and ask: **'how can I use my past pain for my purposes now** and see myself as advantaged *because* of what's happened to me?' It may sound like a crazy idea, but this is precisely what many high achievers do. They decide to look at a situation as life happening FOR them rather than something bad happening TO them.

She decided to use it as leverage — as a launchpad - rather than succumb any more to feeling like a victim.

Look at what happened to Oprah Winfrey. As a child, her grandmother told her she better learn how to handwash clothes because that was part of her future. A 'family friend' raped her and got her pregnant as a teenager. As an adult she over-ate for years as an apology for her incredible success until she realised that she didn't need to do that anymore. These experiences influenced who Oprah became but she did not let them determine her future. **You can do the same – just like Dani did too.**

> ### Dani's Superpower is:
> **I can go through dark times and come out on a mission to make the world a better place.**

Well so can you! Because of your past difficulties and current challenges, you can relate with others in the same boat: you know what it's like! Rewrite the meaning.

What was life trying to teach you? To...

*Be more empathic?
*Be a better parent?
*Be a role model, spokesperson, or advocate?
*Be a leader to others - your clients?
*Give you a clear sense of purpose?
*Be Dani
*Be Oprah
*Be YOU!

When you help your advisors face and rebuttal these demons, it is going to be scary for them! And this is NORMAL – it's the same path everyone goes on. Dani told me: "I think that's how it feels to take ownership of your own life."

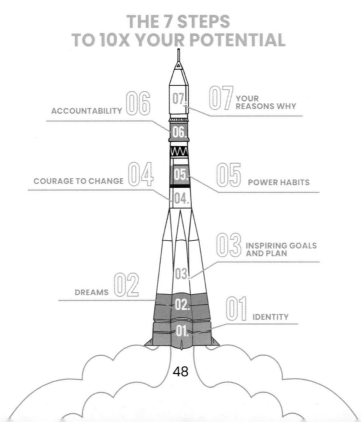

THE 7 STEPS
TO 10X YOUR POTENTIAL

ACCOUNTABILITY 06
07. 07 YOUR REASONS WHY
06.
COURAGE TO CHANGE 04
05. 05 POWER HABITS
04.
03 INSPIRING GOALS AND PLAN
03.
DREAMS 02
02.
01 IDENTITY
01.

CHAPTER 5

What This Other Coventry Lad Surprisingly Does

"You can do anything, but not everything. Set your priorities and focus on what matters."
– Karen Lamb

"The key is not to prioritize what's on your schedule, but to schedule your priorities."
– Stephen Covey

I lived in Coventry in the UK until I was 24. Some years ago, I met a financial advisor called Asvin who had also grown up there at the same time I did. He came up to me after a workshop I ran at the Personal Finance Society conference in Birmingham (UK) and said: "I've been in business for 24 years. For the last seven, I've achieved Court of the Table, but I've never made it to Top of the Table. Do you think you could help me get there?"

Top of the Table is the elite level at the Million Dollar Round Table, the most revered organization in the world of life insurance. I asked him the question I ask every new client: "What type of person do you need to be to make it to TOT?" He thought about it and said: "I need to be more consistent. I have great months and then other things seem to come along and distract me."

I told him: "What you need is what I call a Power Habit to prove to your brain that you're becoming increasingly consistent. A Power Habit leverages the 80-20 Law (the Pareto Principle that 80% of your results come from 20% of your activities): it gets you a significantly skewed outcome for the time you put in. This is an activity you do week-in and week-out whether you feel like it or not. **What's the most important activity you need to be consistent with – and how can you measure it?"**

He looked over his numbers in recent years and replied: "I need to increase my average number of meetings from five to seven. If I can do that, I'm sure I can make Top of the Table."

For the next twelve months, we talked every Monday for thirty minutes. Every week. The same commitment. It wasn't sexy or fascinating. It was consistent.

Most weeks he fell short of seven and sometimes it was hard to see where it was all taking him. But there was no judgement and his consistency paid off. Even though he ended up averaging 6.5 meetings/week, he exceeded his goal by an additional 21%.

More importantly, he has exceeded it for the nine years since in an *increasingly upward trajectory*.

Identify Your Power Habits

Here's how to talk this through with your advisors:

First make sure you're clear from chapter 1 about what type of person you need to be so you can be/do/have what you want in the upcoming months.

Then your next step is to look over your 12-week goals and see if one of them could be a Power Habit.

What's the <u>most important</u> activity YOU need to be consistent with – and how can you measure it?

Is there one that will get you the biggest bang for your buck - help you get to feeling the way you want to feel a year from now?

Have one or two

for your professional life and one or two for your personal life – no more.

If your focus is on prospecting and referrals, the best power habit is to **make a certain number of specific asks per week** – usually five (and sometimes three for more seasoned professionals). If you knock on enough of the right doors, sooner or later ever better opportunities will come.

Another option is to **commit to making 'stretch' asks** – by your own subjective definition an ask that gives you butterflies. These take longer to come to fruition (9 months+) but can be very powerful at helping you go bigger with their business.

Power habits to be increasingly healthy:

*Consistent workouts are going to leverage the 80-20 Law or

*A diet of mostly veggies, protein, and fruit

Power Habits for more love or delight in key relationships:

*A weekly date night with your partner or one of your children will have a much bigger positive impact.

An alternate way to arrive at your power habit is to answer the question that Gary Keller wrote about in his book *The One Thing*: *"What's the one thing I can do such that by doing it everything else will be easier or unnecessary?"* This helps you focus on the most important goal you've set.

What's Your One Thing?

Keller discovered the power of this when the board of his real estate firm reduced a brainstormed list of 100 ways they could grow their company all the way to down to 'One Thing': they decided that Keller should write a book about how to make $1m/year selling residential real estate. The book was so popular that it helped to catapult the firm to #1 in the USA as Realtors from other companies jumped ship to join them believing Keller Williams could do a better job helping them make $1m/year more easily.

The premise of the One Thing is that you will become far more successful by spending your time on fewer things and doing what you do best. His power habit was to time block four hours/day to do what mattered most (which at first was to write his book) and guard that time with all his might. He recommended the same habit to his readers as well.

What ONE THING can you do such that by doing it everything else will be easier or unnecessary?

Now you can look at a power habit. Is it a time allocation to work on the big goal or something you can do daily in smaller chunks?

When you can only focus on ONE thing, your answers may surprise you because you can't lean on the crutch of the laundry list of possible next steps.

What I've learned since I read this book in 2013 is that **it may take you many attempts before you really are clear about your One Thing.**

Another metaphor in the book that explains how your ONE thing adds up over time is the domino effect. Once you start with the right question, your focus and actions accumulate. Step by step these actions build MOMENTUM to create exponential results not incremental ones. And Keller did it himself by co-founding Keller Williams and building what became the largest real estate agency in the USA at the time.

Apply an extreme version of the 80-20 Law to your focus. Whether that means spending much more time with your top six referral sources or top three clients who are most likely to refer you, stop trying to convert 80% of the people you know to refer you – it's a waste of time.

You only want 3-4 Power Habits for your life at any one time. You want to make it easy to focus on what matters most. When your day gets thrown off by the common unexpected events, it is the Power Habit that gets priority.

A couple of tips about power habits for your advisors:

a) **WATCH OUT! Routines can feel dull after a while but must be maintained:** It's like the Olympic swimmer who joked: "I only have to swim twice: When I feel like it and when I don't." We all have a need for the interesting and the new. **You need to quiet the voice trying to persuade you to add variety when you already have a great recipe.** We can unwittingly take our eye off the very habit that is getting us to where we want to go.

b) WATCH OUT! Your lack of worthiness creates self-doubt: rather like a ship starting to steer in a new direction, what's been normal and comfortable for your thinking will be challenged as you start to sense ever better results. This can prompt warning signals from your brain saying: "This direction is unfamiliar. Are you sure you know what you're doing?" (Create a new positive meaning around that if you haven't already – revisit Chapter 4)

This is why your advisors worked on their identity first in Chapter 1: "I am a high performer. This is who I am. Get on with it."

This is why they worked on their new empowered meanings from Chapter 4: "This is my purpose in life. Yes, I deserve to be on this new path."

Your advisors MUST identify their power habits. Without any doubt it is the consistent implementation of these that I have seen from past clients that leads to outstanding outcomes. This is where the 'money' is.

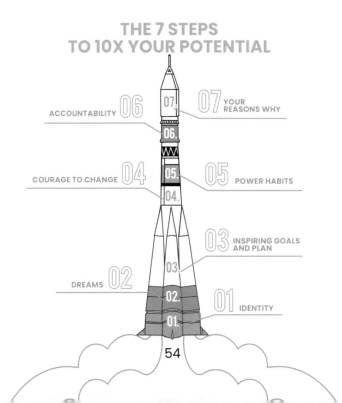

THE 7 STEPS
TO 10X YOUR POTENTIAL

ACCOUNTABILITY 06

07 YOUR REASONS WHY

COURAGE TO CHANGE 04

05 POWER HABITS

03 INSPIRING GOALS AND PLAN

DREAMS 02

01 IDENTITY

CHAPTER 6

The Critical Task

> *"It is not only what we do, but what we do not do,*
> *for which we are accountable."*
> *– Moliere*
>
> *"High performance, highly successful people take*
> *total responsibility for every outcome in their life.*
> *They never make excuses. They look to themselves*
> *for being the cause of situations—they don't blame*
> *other people or other things."*
> *– Grant Cardone*

Now your advisors know how to choose their identity, target how they want to feel, set inspiring goals, keep their new meanings top of mind and identify one-two key power habits, now you want to make sure they track these and create accountability for them.

Many people run away from accountability because they fear it will make them feel like a failure. Here are some ways to resolve this:

55

1. **Agree on measures to report back on.**

   What are the most important metrics to keep track of? This doesn't have to be a laundry list.

   Start with the Power Habits that likely focus on meeting count, prospecting outreach, and/or referral requests/specific asks. Are there key behaviours that would make the biggest positive difference to their results? You can always review frequently based on momentum.

2. **Consider daily questions.**

   Marshall Goldsmith tells a story in his book *Triggers* about a high-performing executive at a Fortune 100 company. The CEO was getting glowing reports from his direct reports about his progress at work but was so frazzled by the end of the workday, he was getting home and spending his evenings arguing with his wife and yelling at his kids.

   "How is it you get to be a consummate professional at work but an amateur at home?" needled Goldsmith. This then prompted his client to add a new daily question to his Habit Tracker: *On a scale of 1-10, did I do my best to be a loving and patient husband and father today?*

   When I read this story, it hit a nerve for me. While I wasn't doing *that badly* at home, I'd be lying if I said I my patience wasn't running out 30-60 minutes *before* my children's bedtime – the time when they were most likely to drag their feet and not comply with my need for peace and no to-do items!

Daily questions have several benefits *especially for identities that do not have tangible targets.* They help your advisors get better and adjust faster to change.

These questions **are Goldsmith's secret weapon with the Fortune 100 CEOs he coaches.** And *if the questions are good enough for them, they are good enough for you and your team* – especially for qualitative areas that are not easy to measure. **Pick and choose which questions sound useful and experiment with them.**

All the questions start with: **Did I do my best to...**

Here are his standard six 'foundation' questions.

On a scale of 1–10, did I do my best to...

1. Set clear goals today?
2. Make progress toward my goals today?
3. Find meaning today?
4. To be happy today?
5. Build positive relationships today?
6. Be fully engaged today?

Did I do my best to... injects personal responsibility and ownership into the questions.

It's not easy *"to face the reality of our own behaviour – and our own effort level – every day."* Especially when we have told ourselves it is something important. So, either we push ourselves into action or we abandon the question. At some point the questions increase our engagement in that area too.

3. Have your advisors partner up with an accountability buddy.

This is powerful. Most people are not effective holding themselves to task on their own – not for long anyway. Even Marshall Goldsmith had someone call him every day for his scores because after long days, he was tired, and his self-discipline was depleted.

4. Have your advisors involve their own stakeholders

This is another gem that Goldsmith finds helps people be more engaged and accountable: have your advisors choose their own stakeholders. Goals have bigger impacts when your team members have their partner, children, mentors, peers, and managers cheering them on and providing feedback.

This is a monthly process that includes telling the stakeholders about their goals and the changes they want to make and asking for ideas (not criticism) on how to make these changes (without commenting on their merits). Ideally your advisors learn from everyone around them.

5. Get them to use a Habit Tracker

I am a HUGE fan of tracking. There are many benefits to remind your advisors about including the frequent dopamine hits, proof that they are doing their best, alignment with the seven steps, and the boosts to self-respect, self-worth, confidence, and results.

Here's how to direct your advisors: Look at the picture of the Habit Tracker at the start of this chapter.

a) Across the top, write in your top 1-2 identities.
b) Then you'll notice the months of the year across the top and the days of the month below that.
c) The next thing I'd draw your attention to is in the bottom half of the tracker: "Power Habits." If you only write in 1-2 habits, this is the place to start and these are the most important, remember? If you're uncertain, you can't go wrong with the key 1-2 professional habits and at least one relating to exercise.
d) Returning to the top half, this is where you can put your 12-week goals to track or other 'supporting' daily habits and daily questions. I'd urge you to write your FEELING words on the left in the margin to remind you why something is on your tracker. Try to keep it simple.
e) Some habits you might simply put an X in if you get it done. Others might be better suited by a number score depending on whether you're measuring yourself in some way.
f) In the bottom half there is also room for weekly and monthly habits.

The best advice I can give is to EXPERIMENT with what you put on your tracker and **make sure it feels good to use.** Having just five focus areas with your inspiring goals should help you avoid trying to change too many parts of your life at once.

You're much better off starting with 3-5 things on your tracker and growing from there if you want to.

If you're scared to start tracking, I do understand AND *just start*. Start tracking one thing and when you feel ready, add to your list.

Handling Advisors' Obstacles to Tracking

What do you do when tracking feels like too much *right now* or you've fallen off the wagon?

Both are common occurrences. These are your options:

i. **Look in the mirror. Choose your hard.**

    Tracking your habits and results is hard; Going too easy on yourself for fear you might feel badly about yourself (and living with mediocre outcomes) is hard.

    Our egos can convince us of all sorts of nonsense and when we don't track or pay close attention to our habits and outcomes, it's scary how well we can fool ourselves into how we spend our time and the choices we make.

ii. **Reduce or pause your tracking and put in a calendar reminder to revisit when to resume.**

    Sometimes it is necessary and healthy to take a break because of a 'lifequake' that demands much of your energy. I understand. I've had them too: I've lost a parent, had twins, and been immobile with back pain that required surgery. I've also experienced what felt like cumulative failure. Elton John was in rehab for a while. Dani was bedridden for four months. But be careful:

60

sometimes what we need even more at times like that is a deeper purpose to help us keep our eyes on the prize.

iii. **When you've fallen off the wagon** and you do check back, look in the mirror please! It's too easy to fool yourself in your comfort zone of not being accountable. Yes, life feels easier but:

Are you getting the same strong results or trajectory you had when you were tracking? Perhaps if a certain habit stuck, your results are good, but otherwise it's highly unlikely.

Yes, you may have lived successfully off your old mojo for a while, but it's not a long-term plan for success and you know this. Those fumes are getting thinner.

iv. **We all do better with accountability – and this is something high achievers who become the stars understand better than anyone.**

So HOW you think about your tracker is really important: See it as a TOOL to SERVE YOU. Nothing else. It's NOT meant to be something that makes you feel rotten about yourself.

Many people I coach do not stick with using a habit tracker for various reasons. Some people don't want to use a hard copy. Some prefer apps. Some use spreadsheets. Others use their electronic calendars and schedule their habits. Some experience early 'failure' and are wary to return to it because of negative association. Some recoil at the sight of what feels like too much structure. And I would still argue it is a priceless tool to stick with the vast majority of the time. Each of us does best with a different amount of structure. Some will help you mine your gold sooner.

It helps to understand the power of positive neurochemicals (such as dopamine) to your brain and feeling good. It's important to be personally vested in the identities you come up with and emotionally tied to what you came up with in chapter 3. The more you want to become that type of person, the more you will want to follow through on making change.

Again, get your advisors to see the tracker as their servant and friend: as positive reinforcement for doing the right thing. Tell them that if they do it for a few months, they will be extremely pleased with all the little things that are cumulatively getting them ever better results!

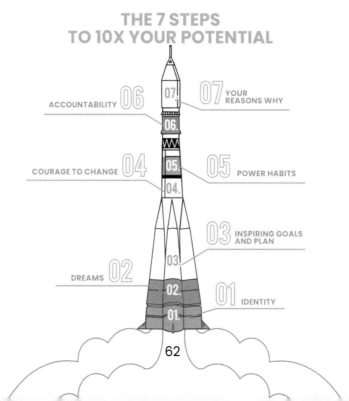

THE 7 STEPS
TO 10X YOUR POTENTIAL

ACCOUNTABILITY 06

07 YOUR REASONS WHY

COURAGE TO CHANGE 04

05 POWER HABITS

03 INSPIRING GOALS AND PLAN

DREAMS 02

01 IDENTITY

CHAPTER 7

The Often-Misunderstood Ignition Method

> *"Your purpose in life is to find your purpose and give your whole heart and soul to it."*
> *– Gautama Buddha*
>
> *"Somewhere, right at the bottom of one's own being, one generally does know where one should go and what one should do. But there are times when the clown we call 'I' behaves in such a distracting fashion that the inner voice cannot make its presence felt."*
> *- Carl Jung*

Henry Peterson was a talented (American) football player at his Virginia high school in the 1920's. He wanted to keep on playing in college and most wanted to play at Georgetown University for Lou Little who was the most prestigious coach of the era. Unfortunately, when he got there, he found himself to be  a small fish in a big pond surrounded by many even better athletes. As a result, he spent his four years of college sitting on the reserve bench and never getting into games.

He was well regarded by Coach Little who often praised him in public as a role model to everyone because he always gave his best. "He's the glue that holds this team together." In his final season Georgetown were having their best year ever and when it came to the last game of the season, they had a chance to win the division championship against Fordham University.

For Henry Peterson it turned out to be a very different week because he received news that his father had died. He went to talk to his coach about what he should do because he didn't want to let his team down. Coach Little told him: "Family is far more important than sports will ever be. Please, you must go home and be there for your family. And here's what we will do, we will put your father's initials on the sleeves of our jerseys and say a prayer for him every day after practice."

Coach Little was true to his word and honoured Peterson's father every day while Henry went home and consoled his younger brothers, sisters, and mother.

On the day of the big game, Little was sitting in his office thinking through final strategy for the game when to his amazement who should walk through the door but Henry Peterson all kitted up and ready to play. "What are you doing here Henry? Why aren't you taking care of your family?"

Peterson replied: "I was there for them all week. I gave them my best, but I had to come here today. Coach, can I ask you a favour?"

"Anything Henry, what?"

"I want to start today's game," requested Peterson.

"Well, Henry when I said anything, I didn't mean *anything*. This game's more important than you and me," was Coach Little's reply. "You've been sitting on my bench for four years; I just can't put you in – there's a lot riding on this game."

Henry implored: "Coach: put me in there and if I make one mistake, you can take me out for the rest of the game."

Coach Little reluctantly agreed. By playing position, Peterson was a running back which meant it was his job to carry the ball downfield and, usually after many attempts, cross the goal line to score. To run for 100 yards is similar to scoring 100 runs playing cricket; it's fairly rare and is considered an outstanding performance. That day Peterson ran for 171 yards and 3 touchdowns (equivalent of three goals in football or hockey). Georgetown won the game, and the championship and Peterson was mobbed by his teammates.

Half amazed and half upset, Coach Little ran up to him and said, "Henry, I had no idea you were that good! I could have used you these past four years! What happened?"

Peterson said: "Did you ever meet my father?"

Little: "No, I wish I had. I saw you walking with him on campus a couple of times but regrettably no, I never did. Why?" asked Coach Little.

"Coach," said Henry, "my father was blind, and today was the first time he ever got to see me play."

That week Henry Peterson didn't magically get faster and stronger, that day he played with a totally different sense of purpose. In his mind it was the first and only chance his father would ever get to watch him play football. It was unacceptable for him not to shine.

Inspiring stories like this are often misunderstood. They are not meant to simply make us feel good for a few fleeting moments. They are meant to be examples for you and me to demonstrate that we have no idea what we are capable of and that when we "play full out" with an inspired sense of purpose, with a new meaning or chosen destiny – with inspired reasons – we can move mountains.

And while it is a story that brings tears to our eyes, what really matters here is

how inspiring are your advisors' reasons to achieve what they want?

How inspiring can they make their purpose?

And how can they maintain this as best as possible on most days when their motivation often fluctuates for its multiple reasons?

This final step is about adding one more powerful injection of fuel to propel your advisors to the greatest heights they want to hit.

List Your Reasons and Your Anchor

Talk your team through these:

a) What are Your Reasons Why?

Start to list them out. This isn't really about the quantity as much as the compelling nature of your reasons to think of when you are not following through. What is most important to you?

*Support your family

*More opportunities for your children

*Nicer home

*Better health

*Financial security/freedom

*Fulfil your potential

*Make your parents proud?

*To *feel* a certain way (joy?)

*What else?

The more jugular your reasons, the better. This list alone might be enough!

b) **Can You Make Your Love Greater Than Your Fear?**

Whether the love is purely from your heart or from a higher power as The Source of Love, could it lead the charge?

In my *5 Habits to Mine Your Gold* book, I wrote that there are only two states of being: love (executive brain) and fear (survival brain). **We either act from a place of love, creativity, and inspiration or from a survival fear-based state**.

The only fear you have is the fear that you are not loveable.

This is a fear created by your ego and this fear holds you back.

One of your reasons why and one of your beliefs can be: "I am loveable, so I can pursue what I love without fear of what happens."

c) **Can You Make Your Purpose Greater Than Your Fear?**

"What is the use of living, if it be not to strive for noble causes and to make this muddled world a better place for those who will live in it after we are gone?
– Winston Churchill

Identifying your purpose in life can be a long journey requiring much reflection and it might change for you over the years. The exercise in Chapter 4 may have helped solve that for you. Other places to start can include:

*Love
*Faith
*Cause
*Serving 'Your' People

- and you only need one of these!

d) Can You Identify Your Anchor Moment?

Henry Peterson went on to have a great career in sales. He called his experience playing in the championship game as his "sweet spot in time" and he used it again and again to have a successful career. Earlier you may recall that Payal Kadakia called her early magical dance experience her "anchor moment." She said that: "Nothing else in my life could compare to it and once I uncovered that, I always wanted to feel that in anything I did." These experiences are the same thing!

You have had anchor moments as well. What do I mean? It was one of those times when you felt like you were on fire. Your confidence was through the roof. For however long it lasted – even if it was only an hour - that day nobody could stop you. You were in a total state of flow. Can you remember it?

For me it was a rugby practice at the Memorial Park when I was 15 and I scored three tries – two of which were the best I ever scored in my six years of playing. It was if another being took over my body that afternoon and I was unstoppable. I have had a few speaking events like this when I got "on a roll," was loose and funny. You have your own version of this.

Unfortunately - all too often - you may have written it off as a fluke - as luck or chance. As something that happened seemingly out of nowhere. It may have never occurred to you that **you can use that moment as an anchor like Henry Peterson and Payal**

Kadakia did to seat in your heart or soul and to turn it on for important situations.

Hearing that this is exactly how they used theirs, now you too can take that anchor seriously and 'cue' that feeling whenever you want to for a key meeting or event. Use your imagination to get you into that state of mind. Why not? Picture it, relive it and do it again.

Your advisors' reasons why matter a LOT. The more jugular their reasons, the better. When they have compelling reasons why, they will spend as long as it takes to figure out HOW they are going to get where they need to go. These reasons can be the final impetus that they need to help them get to the top of your next mountain. They turn the seven steps into a continuous movement as they scale the summit and start to go down into the next valley for their next big challenge.

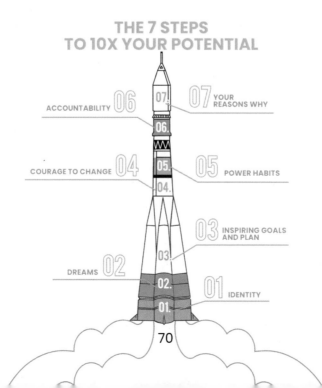

THE 7 STEPS
TO 10X YOUR POTENTIAL

ACCOUNTABILITY 06 07 07 YOUR REASONS WHY

COURAGE TO CHANGE 04 05 05 POWER HABITS

03 INSPIRING GOALS AND PLAN

DREAMS 02

01 IDENTITY

Seven Steps to Fulfil Their Potential

Any one of these seven steps can change the trajectory of one of your advisors' sales paths. A new identity fully invested in can mean it's unacceptable not to be that powerhouse from now on. The right dreams can keep them awake at night figuring out how they can make them happen. Inspired by wanting to feel their best can drive them to do the necessary work to attain those 10X goals. Making new meaning of past obstacle areas can provide the courage to change. The right Power Habits help them focus on doing what matters most – day in and day out. Tracked well and fuelled by compelling reasons – great things are ahead!

I wish you every success!

Matt

P.S. If you want further support with this, you can find me here:

Matt@10xyp.com

LinkedIn: MattAndersonIntl

www.10xyp.com

About the Author

International bestselling author Matt Anderson helps financial advisors maximize their earnings and life potential.

 His results-driven approach has made him a sought-after speaker to audiences from over 40 countries. His clients include financial advisors from 15 different countries, some of whom are now seven-figure earners.

Matt is the author of four books including *Fearless Referrals*, which Brian Tracy, author of *The Psychology of Sales*, says "teaches you the "Golden Rules" for developing a continuous chain of high-quality referrals for any product in any business", and *The 5 Habits to Mine Your Gold*, a comprehensive GPS to fulfil your potential, endorsed by New York Times bestsellers Marshall Goldsmith, B.J. Fogg and Robert Holden.

He has spoken at dozens of national and international industry events including Million Dollar Roundtable, BACK2Y (UK), Personal Finance Society (UK), and HSBC's Global Wealth Management Conference. He has twice been a guest on leading podcasts like Salesman.com, the worlds most downloaded sales podcast and Mario Porreca's Ten Minute Mindset.